Courageous Love
for teens

A Bible Study on Holiness for Young Women
by Stacy Mitch with Emily Stimpson

*"To my daughters,
Elizabeth and Maria."*

Courageous Love for teens

A Bible Study on Holiness for Young Women
by Stacy Mitch with Emily Stimpson

EMMAUS
ROAD
PUBLISHING

Steubenville, Ohio
A Division of Catholics United for the Faith
www.emmausroad.org

Emmaus Road Publishing
827 North Fourth Street
Steubenville, Ohio 43952

Library of Congress Control Number: 2012944018
ISBN: 978-1-937155-82-7

Cover design by Valerie Pokorny
Layout design by Theresa Westling

CONTENTS

INTRODUCTION

Religion isn't about rules. It's about love. It's about the incredible, eternal, unchanging love the all-powerful God of the universe has for you, His precious daughter. And it's also about the love you give back to Him.

God's love, however, isn't some soft, easy, warm fuzzy kind of love. It's a love that wants the very best for you, that seeks to transform you, and that has suffered, sacrificed, and died for you. Because God loves you like that, the love you give back to Him can't be some vague feeling of affection. God doesn't want from you the same kind of love you give to your cat. He wants your whole heart, your whole mind, your whole life.

When you give God that kind of love, you allow Him to give you all the graces you need to become the woman He created you to be. In that love, you become more and more like Christ, the human face of God's love. You become truly happy. You become holy.

As you'll learn in this Bible study, holiness is what God wants for all His children, including you. It's the only path there is in this world to real and lasting joy. And that path begins with courageous love.

Holiness 101

What is the coolest, most important job you can imagine? Being president of the United States? The CEO of Apple Inc.? A missionary in the jungles of South America?

No matter how cool and important those jobs are, God has a job for you that makes every other job you can imagine look boring and insignificant in comparison. The job? Being a saint.

I know, at first glance it probably seems a lot more fun to be a supermodel than it does to be a saint. But that's only because most of us don't see saints for what they are.

Too often when we think of saints, we think of statues of stone nuns clutching bunches of flowers, or paintings of men and women with halos around their head. We know that those people are in heaven with God, which is great; but, that certainly doesn't seem like much of a job, let alone a job more important than being president.

But guess what? Being a saint has nothing to do with having a halo around your head. Being a saint is about being a prayer warrior for God. It's about being completely and perfectly the woman God made you to be. It's about leading people to truth, to love, and to Jesus. And it's about being a coworker of Christ, helping Him heal the world. What job could be more important than that?

So, when does God want you to start this job? After you're dead, right? Wrong.

God wants you to start becoming a saint now. He wants to use your prayers, your witness, and your actions to change the world today, not in sixty or seventy years. He wants you to become holy in this life. He wants everyone to become holy in this life. Holiness and sainthood aren't supposed to be rare honors bestowed on just a few people. They aren't the Academy Awards of the Christian life. They are the call and the destiny God desires for each of us. It's up to us, however, to answer that call. It's up to us, to accept the job He's offering.

Read

1. In Matthew 19:16–22, what does Jesus say is the surest way to enter into eternal life?

_____

_____

2. In that same passage, what commandments does Jesus tell the young man to obey?

_____

_____

3. What did Jesus tell that young man he needed to do in order to be perfect?

_____

_____

4. What was Jesus really asking of the young man? Why do you think this was so difficult for him?

_____

_____

5. Sometimes we can confuse our ideas of holiness with God's ideas of holiness. This was a problem the religious leaders who lived during Jesus' lifetime had. According to Jesus in Matthew 23:28, how did the Pharisees misunderstand true holiness?

_____

_____

_____

6. God calls all of us to become saints. But answering that call is never easy. What do the following passages tell us about some of the obstacles we'll face on the road to sainthood?

Matthew 19:21–22

1 Peter 5:8

1 John 2:15–16

7. In order to overcome those obstacles, we need God's help. We need His grace. But we also have to do some work to prepare ourselves to receive that grace. According to the following passages, how do we prepare ourselves for holiness?

Sirach 2:1–6

Matthew 6:24

2 Chronicles 7:14

Matthew 5:6

1 Thessalonians 5:4–11

8. Even the greatest saints stumbled on their way to holiness. We should expect to do the same. The good news is that God loves us so much that not even our biggest mistakes can stop Him from loving us. Because of that love, He always wants to help us pick ourselves up and start again. He wants to give us the grace we need to become saints. What does Ephesians 2:4–7 tell us about God's love? How has He shown us that love?

_____

_____

_____

Reflect

1. Think about this—God knew He would create you from the beginning of the world! You are His precious daughter. He has a special plan just for you. What do you think is your mission in life? What choices do you make every day that help you accomplish that mission? What choices do you sometimes make that hinder that mission?

_____

_____

2. Think about the young man who walked away from Jesus because he couldn't give up his riches. Is Jesus asking you to do something that you don't want to do? If so, why do you think you're struggling to obey, and how do you think that affects your ability to love God and other people?

_____

_____

3. You listed above some of the obstacles that get in the way of people answering God's call to sainthood. Can you think of any other obstacles? What are some of the ones that you face on a regular basis?

_____

_____

4. How do you respond to those obstacles? What are some of the things you can do to overcome them?

_____

_____

5. List some of the ways God has shown you how much He loves you. What reasons do you have to trust that He will help you answer His call to sainthood?

_____

_____

_____

Resolve

1. Choose one Catholic saint to be your personal prayer warrior. It could be Saint Joseph, the Blessed Virgin Mary, Saint Thérèse of the Child Jesus, or any one of the thousands of holy witnesses the Church has given us. Whoever it is, ask your prayer warrior every day to intercede for you in heaven and help obtain for you the graces you need to become a saint.

2. The best help God gives us to grow in holiness is the gift of Himself in the Eucharist. If possible, take advantage of that gift by going to Mass on at least one weekday, as well as on Sunday.

3. Set aside an extra fifteen minutes each day for prayer. Talk to God about His will for your life, and ask for His help to overcome the obstacles that keep you from doing His will.

MEMORY VERSE

"Strive for peace with all men, and for the holiness without which no one will see the Lord."
Hebrews 12:14

"We cannot decide to become saints without a great effort of renunciation, of resisting temptations, of combat, of persecution, and of all sorts of sacrifices. It is not possible to love God except at one's own expense."

Blessed Teresa of Calcutta, *Heart of Joy*

Did You Know…?

…That even the woman whom Saint Pius X called, "the greatest saint of modern times"—Saint Thérèse of Lisieux—struggled to believe that she could ever become a saint?

"You know Mother," she wrote in her autobiography, *The Story of a Soul*, "I have always wanted to be a saint. Alas! I have always noticed that when I compared myself to the saints, there is between them and me the same difference that exists between a mountain whose summit is lost in the clouds and the obscure grain of sand trampled underfoot by passers-by."

But although sainthood seemed impossible, Saint Thérèse didn't despair. She kept striving, telling herself, "God cannot inspire unrealizable desires. I can, then, in spite of my littleness, aspire to holiness."

Next time you get discouraged, and sainthood seems out of your reach, just think of Saint Thérèse, the Little Flower, and remember that God calls you to nothing that is impossible. He wants you to be holy and with His grace, you can be!

W O R D P L A Y

If you were reading the New Testament in Greek, instead of seeing the word "holy," you would see the word *hagios*.

Hagios literally means "set apart" or "sanctified." So, to become holy means to become set apart for the Lord. It means to give yourself—your heart, your mind, and your will—to Him.

"Being a saint has nothing to do with having a halo around your head. Being a saint is about being a prayer warrior for God."

The Dignity of Womanhood

"Why do I matter?"

That's a question most of us ask ourselves pretty often. And unfortunately, we don't always come up with the right answer.

Sometimes we think we matter because we're pretty or thin or because we have a boyfriend. Other times we think we matter because we have the right clothes, the right car, or the right group of friends. We also can think we matter when we get good grades in school, do really well at sports, or have the lead in the school play.

At the same time, when we don't have those things or when we don't measure up to our own or someone else's idea of what's pretty or cool, we fall into the trap of thinking that we don't matter. We feel like we're not as good as the other girls in our school or the girls we see in magazines and on TV. We suspect we're missing something, lacking something that makes us important, something that makes us worthy of love.

The Bible, however, gives some very different answers to the question, "Why do I matter?" And unlike the answers we tend to come up with, the Bible's answers are the right ones. They're God's answers. And they reveal the truth about what really makes a woman beautiful, important, and loveable. They reveal the true source of your dignity. They reveal the truth about who you, as a woman, are.

Read

1. The Bible presents two accounts of creation. The first, in Genesis 1, is an overview of the creation of the whole world. The second, in Genesis 2, looks more specifically at the creation of man and woman. In Genesis 1, however, we still learn something very important about men and women. Read Genesis 1:26–27. What do those passages tell us about ourselves?

_____

_____

_____

2. In Genesis 2:18–24, we learn more about the creation of woman. According to Genesis 2:18–20, why did God create Eve?

_____

_____

3. According to Genesis 2:21–23, how was Eve created and what was Adam's response when he saw her for the first time? Why does he call her "woman?"

_____

_____

_____

4. What do the above verses tell us about the dignity and importance of women?

_____

_____

5. Every day, we see dozens of advertisements telling us that we need to spend money to be more physically beautiful—to have clearer skin, thicker hair, a thinner body—and that we will be happier and more worthy of love if we look like the women in the advertisements. Why, according to Proverbs 31:30, are those advertisements wrong?

_____

_____

6. During Jesus' lifetime, women weren't always treated respectfully. Women could not own property. They weren't considered capable of serious learning. They were not allowed to give testimony at a trial because their word wasn't considered reliable. Jesus, however, knew women were created in the image and likeness of God and deserved to be treated with great respect. How do His actions in the following passages demonstrate that?

Mark 5:25–34

Luke 21:1–4

John 4:7–27

John 8:3–11

7. According to the following passages, who was at the foot of the Cross when Jesus was crucified?

Matthew 27:55–66

Mark 15: 40–41

Luke 23:49

John 19:25–26

8. Based on the passages listed above, were the apostles present at the Crucifixion? What does this tells us about the character and strength of women?

_____

_____

9. Saint Paul wrote that the Resurrection is the cornerstone of Christianity and the most miraculous event in history (1 Cor. 15:17). According to John 20:11–18, who first witnessed Jesus' Resurrection? Why might Jesus have chosen to reveal Himself in that way?

_____

_____

_____

Reflect

1. What do you think it means to be a woman?

_____

_____

2. What messages about women's worth and dignity do you see in the current culture? These messages might come through the advertisements you see, the movies you watch, the music you listen to, as well as other places. What messages are positive? What messages are negative?

_____

_____

_____

3. In what ways do those negative messages contradict what Scripture says about the dignity of women?

_____

_____

4. In the past, how have you answered the question, "Why do I matter?" What are some of the wrong answers you're tempted to believe? If you've chosen at times to believe those wrong answers, how has that made you feel? Did believing those wrong answers lead you to make any wrong or foolish choices? If so, what were those choices?

_____

_____

_____

5. Who are the women that you look up to the most? Why? In what ways do they embody the dignity of womanhood depicted in the Bible? What have you learned from them? And what are some practical things you can do to be more like them?

_____

_____

_____

6. Can you think of a time where you loved someone or something as courageously as the women who stood by Jesus during His Crucifixion loved Him? Describe what happened: How did your decision to love courageously make you feel? Where did you find your courage? What happened as a result of your actions?

_____

_____

_____

Resolve

1. Pray the Joyful Mysteries of the Rosary. If you aren't familiar with those mysteries, look them up online. As you pray the mysteries, think about the role Mary played in Jesus' life, what that teaches us about the dignity of women, and how you can better imitate her.

2. Throw out any fashion or beauty magazines you might own that make you feel like your worth is in the way you look or the way you dress.

3. If your friends speak unkindly or unfairly about someone, speak up and defend that person, then redirect the conversation away from gossip.

MEMORY VERSE

"And Mary said, 'Behold,
I am the handmaid of the Lord;
let it be to me according to your word.'"
Luke 1:38

"It has been woman's mission to war against evil, and to educate her posterity to do the same."

Saint Edith Stein, Woman

Did You Know...?

. . . That the Catholic Church is the oldest champion of women's education in the world?

Way back in the fourth century, Saint Jerome taught Greek and Hebrew to women so that they could read the Bible. Later, holy women like the Abbess Hildegard of Bingen (now a Doctor of the Church), wrote major works of philosophy, studied science, composed poetry, and encouraged the nuns in her charge to study science and philosophy as well.

During the Dark Ages, when most of the population of Europe was illiterate, the convents founded by Saint Scholastica, twin sister of Saint Benedict, helped keep learning alive. Later, orders of religious like the Ursulines were founded specifically to educate women.

TRUE OR FALSE?

The Catholic Church doesn't allow women to be priests because it's sexist and believes women are inferior to men.

False!

The Catholic Church believes women and men are both created in God's image and likeness and are equal in dignity. It does not believe women are inferior to men or that they are any less intelligent or capable. Rather, the Church believes that men and women each uniquely image God, and possess special gifts and talents that are reflected in their masculinity and femininity.

When Jesus was on earth, although He worked closely with women in many ways, He appointed only men to be His apostles—to teach, to lead, and to administer the sacraments. These men and their successors—bishops and priests—have a fatherly role in the Church.

Women have a different role. Like Mary, the Mother of God, our advocate and intercessor, it is our special job to be advocates and intercessors for the Church, nurturing spiritual growth through our prayers and acts of service. These two roles—the fatherly role and the motherly role—complement each other. Both are essential and both reflect who we are as men and women.

"When we don't measure up to our own or someone else's idea of what's pretty or cool, we fall into the trap of thinking that we don't matter...We suspect we're missing something, lacking something that makes us important, something that makes us worthy of love."

Faith and the Life of Grace

One of the buzzwords in Hollywood these days is "spiritual." Actors, actresses, rock stars, and models always seem to be telling reporters how "spiritual" they are. Which sounds like a good thing, right? After all, isn't "spiritual" just another way of saying their faith is important to them?

Not exactly.

When people say they're spiritual, it can mean just about anything. It might mean they believe in God . . . or it might not. It might mean they believe there is more to the world than just neutrons, electrons, and protons . . . or it might not. It might mean they believe that something more than feelings (that is, a moral law) should impact the way they treat others . . . or it might not. You just never know with that word. More often than not, it doesn't mean much of anything. Describing themselves as "spiritual" is some people's way of making themselves sound "deep"—a way that doesn't demand anything, that doesn't require tough choices, and that doesn't ask anyone to deny their own desires.

Faith, however, is a whole different ballgame.

Unlike "being spiritual," faith makes demands, and lots of them. But also unlike "being spiritual," when your faith is faith in Christ, it actually does something. It transforms you. Faith in Christ works from the inside out, helping you to become more beautifully and perfectly you. It helps you love better, work harder, give more, and do more. It helps you accomplish what you could never accomplish on your own. It brings lasting peace, lasting joy, and lasting life. Faith helps you become a radiant reflection of Christ.

Makes simply "being spiritual" sound kind of lame, doesn't it?

Read

1. According to Hebrews 11:1, what is "faith"?

_____

_____

2. How does Philippians 1:29 say that faith is acquired?

_____

_____

3. What does Hebrews 11:6 say is the importance of faith?

_____

_____

4. According to Matthew 7:21, is it enough to just profess faith in Christ or is something more required if we want to be counted as citizens of the kingdom of heaven?

_____

_____

5. What does Jesus tell us in John 6:53–54 that we must do to inherit eternal life? When do you do this?

_____

_____

6. Hebrews 11 is sometimes referred to as the Faith Hall of Fame. Read the chapter; then, list the deeds that bore witness to the faith of the following men and women:

Person	Deed or Deeds
Abel	
Enoch	
Noah	
Abraham	
Sarah	
Isaac	
Jacob	
Joseph	
Moses	
The People of Israel	
Rahab	
Gideon, Barak, Samson, Jephthah, David, Samuel, and the prophets	
Women and others	

7. The Bible is filled with other stories of women who showed us what it means to have a living and active faith. Read the stories about these New Testament women; then, answer the questions about their faith.

	Mt. 15:21–28	Mk. 5:24–34	Lk. 1:26–38
What was the woman's faith in?			
How did she show her faith?			
What was God's response to her faith?			
How was her life different because of her faith?			

Reflect

1. Describe your own faith: What is your faith in? What are some of the things your faith asks of you? How do you feel about those demands? How have your feelings changed as you've gotten older?

_____

_____

2. What are some of the things that you say and do that demonstrate that faith? How do your actions bear witness to your faith?

_____

_____

3. Do any of your actions not bear witness to your faith? What are some of the things you might occasionally say or do that don't reflect your belief in God and the love you have for Him?

_____

_____

_____

4. Has your faith ever been tested? If so, how did you respond to that test?

_____

_____

5. Describe an event in your life that has strengthened your faith.

_____

_____

6. How has your faith in God helped you and changed you? How has God responded to your faith and obedience?

_____

_____

Resolve

1. State your faith. Begin your day with this simple prayer. It's called an Act of Faith:

> O my God, I firmly believe that You are one God in three divine Persons, Father, Son and Holy Spirit. I believe that your divine Son became man and died for our sins, and that He will come to judge the living and the dead. I believe these and all the truths that the holy Catholic Church teaches, because You have revealed them, Who can neither deceive nor be deceived.

2. Live your faith.

Resolve to give one extra hour of your time this week to helping someone in need. That could mean raking an elderly neighbor's lawn, babysitting for a young mother, visiting someone in a nursing home, or just doing some extra chores around the house without being asked.

3. Feed your faith.

Read one book about God or a saint this month that is *not* required for school.

MEMORY VERSE

"So Jesus said to them, 'Truly, truly, I say to you,
unless you eat the flesh of the Son of man
and drink his blood, you have no life in you;
he who eats my flesh and drinks my blood
has eternal life, and I will raise
him up on the last day.'"
John 6:53–54

"Faith is to believe what you do not see; the reward of this faith is to see what you believe."

St. Augustine, *Sermones*

THINKING IS BELIEVING

God doesn't want you to check your brain at the church door. He wants you to use the mind He gave you to know more and understand more about Him. There are very good reasons why Catholics believe what they do—reasons supported by philosophy, science, and history, as well as by revelation.

To find out more about the reasons behind your beliefs, visit www.cuf.org and check out the Faith Facts page. There you'll find answers to your own and your friends' toughest questions about the Church.

PLAN ON BECOMING A SAINT?

Then you better plan on practicing the obedience of faith. That means doing the things God and your faith ask of you.

1. Get Baptized

"Jesus answered, 'Truly, truly, I say to you, unless one is born of water and the Spirit, he cannot enter the kingdom of God.'"

John 3:5

2. Go to Confession

"If we confess our sins, he is faithful and just, and will forgive our sins and cleanse us from all unrighteousness."

I John 1:9

3. Receive Communion

"So Jesus said to them, 'Truly, truly, I say to you, unless you eat the flesh of the Son of man and drink his blood, you have no life in you; he who eats my flesh and drinks my blood has eternal life, and I will raise him up on the last day.'"

John 6:53–54

4. Love God

"You shall love the Lord your God with all your heart, and with all your soul, and with all your mind, and with all your strength."

Mark 12:30

5. Love One Another

"This is my commandment, that you love one another as I have loved you."

John 15:12

"Describing themselves as 'spiritual' is some people's way of making themselves sound 'deep'—a way that doesn't demand anything, that doesn't require tough choices, and that doesn't ask anyone to deny their own desires."

Love:
To Serve Is to Reign

"Dare to love."

That is Pope Benedict XVI's challenge to you, a challenge he issued for the 22nd World Youth Day. At first, it seems like kind of a funny challenge, doesn't it? I mean, normally we dare people to do risky or difficult things. We dare them to hold their breath underwater, to climb to the top of a tree, or to ask someone to a dance. But to love? What's so daring about love? We do it all the time. We love our parents, our friends, our pets, even our favorite band. Love seems a pretty common thing, something we do naturally, and certainly not something we have to be dared to do.

But the Holy Father wasn't talking about that kind of love. He wasn't talking about an emotion, a feeling of affection or attraction. He was talking about a love that the world saw for the first time on Calvary, when God Himself hung on a Cross. That love is a love that chooses to love even when love is the most difficult choice imaginable. It is a love that lasts, that remains faithful, that sacrifices and serves. It is also a love that transforms hearts, lives, and entire cultures.

The world likes to tell us that kind of love doesn't exist. That's a lie, but it's a lie we easily believe because we've all seen love fail. We've seen people give up on love in tough times, break their promises, and walk away. That happens because love, real love, is hard. It doesn't come naturally. And it is risky—which brings us back to the Holy Father's challenge.

He dares you to love. He dares you to love your family and your friends. He dares you to love your teachers, strangers at the mall, and the people at school who are not kind to you. He dares you to love God. And he dares you to love all of them with an unchanging, unwavering, unrelenting love that holds nothing back. He dares you to love as God loves you.

Read

1. If we're going to love like God, we need to know more about what His love looks like. Read the following passages. What does each of them tell us about God's love for us?

Jeremiah 31:3

John 17:22-26

Romans 5:8

1 John 3:1–2

2. According to 1 Corinthians 13:1–3, what spiritual gifts and virtues amount to nothing if we "have not love"?

_____

_____

3. What does Saint Paul tell us in 1 Corinthians 13:4–8 about what love looks like? List the characteristics of love that he names.

_____

_____

4. Real love, remember, is more than a feeling. It's a choice. And it's a choice that requires action. What actions do the following verses tell us love requires?

Deuteronomy 10:12–13

Romans 13:8–10

1 John 3:16

5. According to Galatians 5:6, why does love require action?

_____

_____

6. What commandment does Jesus give to His disciples in John 13:34?

_____

_____

7. List at least three examples of how Jesus showed His love for men and women during His life on earth.

_____

_____

8. Read Luke 1:35-38. How does Mary show her love for God in that passage?

_____

_____

Reflect

1. Compare and contrast Hollywood's definition of love with God's definition of love. Give one or two examples of movies about love. How do they depict it? How is their depiction similar to or different from the true meaning of love we find in Scripture?

_____

_____

2. Think back to the characteristics of love from 1 Corinthians 13 that you listed above. Do those characteristics describe the way that you love people? If not, with which ones do you struggle the most?

_____

_____

3. Can you think of one example where you imitated Christ in showing your love for someone? Describe the situation: Was it hard for you to give that kind of love? If so, what helped you overcome that struggle? What happened as a result of your decision? What did you learn from that situation?

_____

_____

_____

4. Name one person who has imitated Christ in how he or she has loved you. How did that person show you that love? How did you receive it? Were you grateful? How did being loved like that change the way you see yourself? How can you imitate that person in your relationships with your friends and family?

_____

_____

_____

5. Mary showed her love for God by saying yes to Him at the Annunciation. What is God asking you to say yes to right now? Are you saying it? If not, why not? What obstacles are getting in the way of your yes? What can you do to remove those obstacles?

_____

_____

_____

6. It's a fact: Jesus knows you better than anyone else knows you, and He loves you more than anyone else loves you. That love is more powerful and more true than any other love you can imagine. Do you ever struggle, however, to believe that fact? Why or why not?

_____

_____

_____

Resolve

1. Work on showing your love for your parents this week by saying yes (without complaining!) whenever they ask for your help.

2. Practice patience. When a sibling or a friend does something annoying, don't say or do anything in response.

3. Pray to the Holy Spirit and ask Him to remove the obstacles getting in the way of your yes to God.

MEMORY VERSE

"It shall not be so among you; but whoever
would be great among you must be your servant,
and whoever would be first among you must be your slave;
even as the Son of man came not to be served but to serve,
and to give his life as a ransom for many."
Matthew 20:26–28

*"We are saved or damned according to what we love. If we love God, we
shall ultimately get God; we shall be saved. If we love self in preference to
God, then we shall get self apart from God; we shall be damned."*

Frank Sheed, Theology and Sanity

De•fin•ing
TERMS

Charity (noun)
    char•i•ty [chárruhtee]
    From the Latin *caritas*
        "The theological virtue by which we love
    God above all things for his own sake, and our
    neighbors as ourselves for the love of God."
            Catechism of the Catholic Church, 1822
    Synonym: Love

Did You Know…?

. . . That when Mary says to the Angel Gabriel, "I am the
handmaid of the Lord," the word for "handmaid" Saint Luke
used in the original Greek version of the passage was *doule?* In
Greek, *doule* means "a female slave." "Slave" is a word that for
many of us conjures up images of chains, oppression, and hate.
But that's not what Mary meant by the word at all.

In calling herself God's *doule*, Mary was saying that God's
will was now her will, and that she was willing to serve Him

at all cost. And God rewarded her for that. Not only did she become the Mother of God, but she became the Queen of Heaven.

Blessed John Paul II once said, in the kingdom of heaven, "to serve is to reign." In other words, Mary took her place in God's kingdom not by being rich or powerful or beautiful, but rather by giving her life to God in service. She shows us that the ideal woman is not a supermodel, but a woman who is completely open to God and whose heart is overflowing with a love that is ready and willing to serve.

"We dare people to hold their breath underwater, to climb to the top of a tree, or to ask someone to a dance. But to love? What's so daring about love?"

Prayer: The Way to a New Heart

Here are a few questions for you: How much time did you spend on the phone last week with your best friends? How many e-mails and text messages did you send them? How often did you chat with them online?

Here's another question: How much time did you spend talking with God last week? Probably not as much time as you spent text messaging, right?

If so, don't feel too bad. It's normal. But, think about what your relationships with your friends would be like if you talked to them a whole lot less than you do. What kind of friendships would you have if you never shared with your friends what was going on in your life? Even more important, what kind of friend would you be to them if you never listened to what they had to say? Those friendships wouldn't be very real, would they?

On a spiritual level, the same holds true for your relationship with God. The more time you spend talking with Him, the closer you'll become. By telling God about all your hopes and struggles, you develop the habit of turning to Him in every moment, of recognizing how much you depend on His guidance and His grace. You develop the habit of listening to God, of quietly waiting to hear His voice. You also learn how to love Him through words of praise and time of silent adoration.

I know, it sounds like an awful lot to learn. But this isn't like the learning that goes on in a classroom. This is like the learning that goes on between two friends getting to know each other or between a man and a woman on the road to marriage. This is learning to love and be loved. And that kind of learning always ends in joy. That's where prayer leads you. It leads you to God. It leads you to joy.

Read

1. According to Ephesians 6:18, how often are we supposed to pray?

_____

_____

2. In Matthew 7:7, what does Jesus tell us we must do? What does He promise will happen if we follow His instructions?

_____

_____

3. What does Deuteronomy 4:29 say we must do to grow closer to God?

_____

_____

4. What does the Lord promise us in Psalm 145:18–19?

_____

_____

5. According to James 5:16, why should we pray for one another? What will make those prayers effective?

_____

_____

6. Learning how to pray isn't a guessing game. Throughout the Bible, God gives us very specific instructions on prayer. In the New Testament, Jesus frequently did this through short stories called "parables." Read the following parables and answer the questions in the table below.

	Luke 11:5–13	Luke 18:1–8	Luke 18:9–14
How are we to pray?			
What is the result of prayer?			

7. Jesus' most specific instructions on prayer actually came in the form of a prayer, the Our Father. That prayer, which you'll find in Matthew 6:9–13, includes the four basic elements of prayer—the four things we should say to God and ask for when we pray. Can you identify those elements?

1. _____

2. _____

3. _____

4. _____

8. During His life on earth, Jesus did more than tell His followers how to pray. He showed them through His own example. Read the following passages that show us Jesus in prayer. As you read, fill in the answers to the questions in the table below.

Mark 1:35
Mark 6:46–47
Luke 5:16
Luke 6:12
Matthew 26:36–45
John 17

	Jesus' Prayer Life
When did Jesus pray?	
How did Jesus pray?	
Where did Jesus pray?	
For what did Jesus pray?	

Reflect

1. Describe your own prayer life: How often do you pray? What do you pray for? Where do you pray? How do you pray?

_____

_____

_____

2. Think back to the elements of prayer Jesus included in the Our Father. Are any of those elements missing in your prayer life? If so, how can you model your own prayers more closely on Jesus' prayer?

_____

_____

_____

3. Think back to a time when God gave you what you asked for in prayer. Describe that instance. How did you feel afterward? How did His response change you and your relationship with Him?

_____

_____

_____

4. Because God knows better than we do what is best for us, His answer to our prayers is sometimes no. Have you ever been grateful that God said no to one of your prayers? If so, what did that experience teach you? How has it changed the way you pray?

_____

_____

_____

5. Prayer doesn't just change situations; it changes people. How has your time spent with God in prayer changed you?

_____

_____

6. Although we often have the best intentions about spending more time in prayer, we're not always able to follow through with those intentions. What are some of the obstacles and distractions that prevent you from giving God the time and attention you want to give Him in prayer? What can you do to overcome those obstacles?

_____

_____

_____

Resolve

1. Be an intercessor. In a journal or notebook, keep a running list of people who need your prayers, and at least once a day, devote some time to praying for their intentions.

2. Carve out an extra fifteen minutes each day to be alone with God.

3. At least once a week, visit a church where you can pray before Jesus in the tabernacle or in a perpetual adoration chapel.

MEMORY VERSE

"The Lord is near to all who call upon him,
to all who call upon him in truth. He fulfils the
desires of all who fear him, he also hears
their cry, and saves them."
Psalm 145:18–19

"We must love prayer. It widens the heart to the point of making it capable of containing the gift that God makes of himself. Ask and seek, and your heart will be widened to welcome him and to keep him within itself."
Blessed Teresa of Calcutta, *Heart of Joy*

Did You Know...?

. . . That there are three different types of Christian prayer,
all of which are essential to a strong prayer life? They are:

1. *Vocal Prayer*: This is the type of prayer most of us are the
   most familiar with. It's called "vocal" because it involves
   your talking to God, but that talking doesn't have to be
   aloud. It can also be silent, your thinking the words in your
   head. Vocal prayers can be informal—for example, your
   taking your petitions to God or praising Him in your own
   words—or it can be formal, praying the Rosary, the Liturgy
   of the Hours, or some other set form of prayer.

2. *Meditative Prayer*: This type of prayer seeks deeper
   understanding of God and the truths of the faith. It involves
   the concentrated attention of your mind on one or more of
   these truths. To help focus your mind or direct its thought,
   you can read a passage from Scripture, the writings of a
   saint, or a book about the faith. You can also look at a
   religious picture, a statue, or an icon and think about what
   truth it reveals.

3. *Contemplative Prayer:* This is a prayer of silence. Saint John Vianney described his experience of contemplative prayer as "I look at Him and He looks back at me." In contemplative prayer, you let the words go, and just sit in God's presence.

NOT SURE WHAT TO SAY?

Prayer doesn't have to be complicated. When you go before God, all you have to do is open your heart to Him and let Him know what's on your mind. You can also pray the prayers God has given to us through His saints in time. The words of these prayers both teach about our faith and help us express ourselves to God.

These prayers can, for example, include:

♦ The Rosary
♦ The Divine Mercy Chaplet
♦ The Liturgy of the Hours
♦ The Divine Praises
♦ The Litany of the Blessed Virgin Mary
♦ The *Memorare*

Give yourself extra credit and learn more about each of these prayers online.

"What kind of friendships would you have if you never shared with your friends what was going on in your life? Even more important, what kind of friend would you be to them if you never listened to what they had to say? Those friendships wouldn't be very real, would they?"

Obedience: The Proof of Our Love

"Because I said so."

How many times has that phrase come out of your parents' mouths? Sometimes, it seems like there are fewer phrases spoken more often by parents than that one. And there are certainly fewer phrases more annoying. When Mom and Dad speak those four little words, it's like running into a brick wall. End of debate. End of discussion. Issue over.

As frustrating as it is to hear those words, there's a reason your parents use them. And it's not because they don't have any better reasons to give you. It's because they are trying to teach you the virtue of obedience. They're trying to teach you that they have your best interests at heart, and that even when you don't understand their rules and decisions, you have to trust them and do what they say. When you obey them, you show you trust them. You also show your love for them.

Obedience to God works a lot like obedience to your parents. There are always reasons for what He asks us to do and for the rules of life He's given to us. But sometimes, those reasons don't seem all that clear. They don't make much sense to our human minds. When that is the case, God wants us to obey anyhow. He wants us to trust that He has our best interests—our eternal happiness—at heart. He wants us to show our love for Him by obeying Him.

When we trust God, when we obey "because He says so," we are never disappointed. We learn, time and again, that He really does know best. And eventually, we also come to understand the reasons behind all that He asks us to do. We learn how to find our way home to heaven.

Read

1. What do Matthew 7:21–27 and 1 John 2:17 tell us will happen if we do the will of God?

_____

_____

2. What does Ephesians 5:5–6 tell us will happen to us if we do *not* do the will of God?

_____

_____

3. In John 14:15, what does Jesus say we will do if we love Him?

_____

_____

4. What does 1 John 5:3 tell us about God's commandments?

_____

_____

5. How, according to John 15:14, do we become Jesus' friends?

_____

_____

6. When we obey God, we know we will be blessed, both in this life and in eternal life. Read the following passages; then, list the blessings each passage promises to those who obey.

	Blessings of Obedience
Isaiah 3:10	
John 15:10–11	
James 1:25	
2 Corinthians 5:10	
1 Peter 5:4	
Revelation 22:12	
Revelation 22:14	

7. Obedience can be hard, not just because it asks us to submit our own will to God's, but also because there are many temptations to disobey. According to James 1:13-15, what is the source of these temptations?

_____

_____

8. According to 1 Corinthians 10:13, if a temptation to disobedience ever feels too powerful to combat, what should we remember?

_____

_____

9. Saying someone has committed a sin is another way of saying someone has been disobedient to God. Sin is not doing what we know we should do, or doing what we know we shouldn't. In the Book of Acts, we read about the sin of Sapphira. Read her story in Acts 5:1-11; then, answer the following questions.

a. Who was Sapphira?_____

b. What was her sin?_____

c. What happened to her as a result of her sin?_____

_____

d. What was Peter's response to Sapphira?_____

_____

Reflect

1. What are some of the things your parents ask you to do that require obedience? Why do you think they ask these things of you? What are the good things that have come from obeying them, even when you haven't really wanted to obey?

_____

_____

_____

2. What are some of the things God asks of you that require obedience? Why do you think He asks these things of you? What are some of the good things that have happened to you when you have obeyed Him?

_____

_____

_____

3. If your parents or friends said they loved you but never did anything to show you that love, their words wouldn't mean much, would they? God feels the same way about our love. He doesn't just want to hear us say we love Him. He wants us to show Him that we love Him through our actions. What are some of the ways you show your love of God through your actions?

_____

_____

_____

4. We obey God because we love Him and we trust that He knows what is best for us. That's why a failure to obey is really a failure to love. What are some of the ways in which you are or have been disobedient to God and failed to show Him the love you have for Him?

_____

_____

_____

5. How can you better use the "weapons" of Scripture and prayer to combat temptations to sin and disobedience?

_____

_____

6. List three practical things you can do this week to show God your love for Him.

1. _____
2. _____
3. _____

Resolve

1. Go to Confession this week.
2. Memorize this prayer. Pray it at least once a day and whenever a temptation to sin strikes.

> *Saint Michael the Archangel, defend us in battle. Be our protection against the wickedness and snares of the devil. May God rebuke him, we humbly pray, and do thou, O Prince of the heavenly hosts, by the power of God, cast into hell Satan and all the evil spirits who prowl about the world seeking the ruin of souls.*

3. Try to get through a whole week without questioning your parents' instructions and making them use the phrase "Because I said so."

MEMORY VERSE

"For this is the love of God,
that we keep his commandments.
And his commandments
are not burdensome."
1 John 5:3

"Love, daughters, must not be fabricated in our imaginations but proved by deeds. And don't think He needs our works; He needs the determination of our wills."

Saint Teresa of Avila, The Interior Castle

BATTLE PLAN

Sin isn't just a battle against ourselves and our own will. It's a battle against Satan. Satan hates us. He hates you. And the last thing he wants is for you to spend an eternity of joy with God. That's why in Ephesians 6:12, Saint Paul writes:

"For we are not contending against flesh and blood, but against the principalities, against the powers, against the world rulers of this present darkness, against the spiritual hosts of wickedness in the heavenly places."

So how do you fight this battle? How do you, a teenage girl, take on the Prince of Darkness?

Saint Paul lays out your plan for battle in Ephesians 6:13–18.

"Therefore take the whole armor of God, that you may be able to withstand in the evil day, and having done all, to stand. Stand therefore, having fastened the belt of truth around your waist, and having put on the breastplate of righteousness, and having shod your feet with the equipment of the gospel of peace; besides all these, taking the shield of faith, with which you can quench all the flaming darts of the Evil One. And take the helmet of salvation, and the sword of the Spirit, which is

the word of God. Pray at all times in the Spirit, with all prayer and supplication. To that end keep alert with all perseverance, making supplication for all the saints."

In other words: know the Truth; live the Truth; learn the Scriptures; and above all, pray.

Did You Know...?

. . . That some of the Church's greatest saints were once some of the world's greatest sinners?

Saint Augustine, the great Doctor of the Church, was an atheist for years and lived with a woman who was not his wife. Saint Teresa of Avila, mystic and reformer of religious life in the sixteenth century, spent much of her early years in the convent thinking about clothes and wishing she was elsewhere. Saint Francis of Assisi, as a young man, partied more than prayed.

Heaven is full of people who disobeyed God on a grand scale. But none of their sins was too big for God to forgive. God loves you and wants your love in return. No matter how much you've disobeyed Him in the past, it's not too late to ask for His forgiveness and change your ways. Don't let Satan convince you otherwise.

When we trust God, when we obey 'because He says so,' we are never disappointed. We learn, time and again, that He really does know best."

Purity: The Way to See God

Have you ever worn someone else's eyeglasses? If not, try it. The world, as you normally see it, will change. Some objects will appear bigger. Others smaller. Shapes will stretch, contract, and fold in on themselves. You won't recognize the most familiar objects. Everything will be distorted, blurred, wrong. If you try to walk, you'll fall or bump up against something. You will have lost your bearings, your ability to navigate through the world around you.

Did you know that sin does exactly the same thing to your spiritual vision that the wrong eyeglass prescription does to your physical vision? It corrupts how you understand truth. It blurs your vision of God, yourself, and others. It distorts your whole view of reality.

But what's even more frightening about sin, is that sin does its damage slowly, incrementally. You don't realize how much your vision is changing. You don't realize that the picture of reality you see is distorted. And when you fall, you fall all the harder and faster for that.

Unfortunately, getting your spiritual vision back to how it should be isn't as easy as taking off a pair of eyeglasses. That's why the best way to ensure you see God and the world properly is to avoid sin in the first place, to keep your heart and mind pure. But, even if you've let sin begin to damage your vision, it's never too late to correct it. The more damage done, the longer this will take, but by seeking purity and by calling on God for help, you really can get your vision back.

Read

1. How does Psalm 24:3–6 define purity?

_____

_____

2. Why, according to 2 Timothy 2:21 should we seek purity?

_____

_____

3. In Matthew 5:8, what blessing does Jesus promise we will receive if we are "pure of heart"?

_____

_____

4. How, according to Psalm 73:1, does God treat the pure of heart?

_____

_____

5. What does Job 8:5–6 say that God will do for those who are pure?

_____

_____

6. What must we do, according to Colossians 3:5, to regain the purity we've lost through sin?

_____

_____

7. What other advice about becoming pure does Saint John give us in 1 John 3:2–3?

_____

_____

8. In Psalm 119:9, we learn that God has given us a tool to help us in our quest for purity. What is that tool?

_____

_____

9. Your feminine beauty is a gift from God. As the image of God, you reflect the beauty of God in a very special and powerful way. Beauty is a blessing. It can also be a temptation to impurity for men. And, if it's a man to whom you're attracted, his temptation can quickly become your temptation. That means, like it or not, you have the special responsibility of guarding both men and yourself from that temptation.

Read the following verses. What advice do they give about how women should dress and act in order to uphold purity?

1 Timothy 2:9–10

1 Peter 3:1–4

Titus 2:3–5

Reflect

1. Scripture promises us that if we remain faithful to the end, we will one day see God face-to-face. When that day comes, what kind of heart do you want to present to God? What kind of life do you need to lead in order to give Him that kind of heart?

_____

_____

2. How has sin damaged your vision? Have you made compromises with what you know is right and then justified those compromises in any way? How has that affected your relationship with God?

_____

_____

3. The culture we live in is full of temptations to impurity. From pornography to suggestive advertisements and music, these temptations can make it almost impossible for us to guard our minds against sin. What temptations to impurity do you encounter on a regular basis?

_____

_____

4. How can you better avoid those temptations? What steps can you take to guard against them?

_____

_____

5. Think about the clothes hanging in your closet. Is there anything in your closet that shouldn't be there, that you know is immodest? If so, what? What makes those clothes immodest? Also, why are they in your closet? What tempts you to wear them? Do you need to rethink the way that you dress?

_____

_____

6. Modesty isn't just about what we wear, it's also about how we act. List what actions you think could be considered immodest behavior. Have you ever been guilty of that kind of behavior? If so, what led you to act that way? How can you act differently in the future?

_____

_____

Resolve

1. Go shopping for tank tops, T-shirts, cardigans, and leggings that you can wear under or over any shirts, dresses, and skirts you own that push the boundaries of modesty.

2. Go online and learn more about Saint Maria Goretti. Ask for her intercession when you face temptations to impurity.

3. Avoid watching movies that glamorize sexual impurity. When you can't, leave the room during an inappropriate scene, avert your eyes, or ask whoever else is present if you can fast-forward to the next scene.

MEMORY VERSE

"Whom have I in heaven but you?
And there is nothing upon earth that I desire besides you.
My flesh and my heart may fail, but God is the strength
of my heart and my portion forever."
Psalm 73:25–26

"Blessed are the clean in heart, for they shall see God' (Mt. 5:8). A man is really clean of heart when he has no time for the things of this world, but is always searching for the things of heaven, never failing to keep God before his eyes and always adoring him with a pure heart and soul."

Saint Francis of Assisi, The Admonitions

De•fin•ing
TERMS

Purity (noun)
  pur·i·ty [pyóoruhtee]
    1. freedom from contaminants
    2. innocence
    3. clarity
    4. correctness

Modesty (noun)
   Mod·es·ty [módduhstee]
      1. humility
      2. sexual reserve
      3. simplicity
      4. moderation

TRUE OR FALSE?

Dressing modestly means dressing unfashionably and looking frumpy.

False!

Modesty is not a synonym for frumpy. It doesn't mean dressing like your mother or grandmother. It means dressing in such a way that you don't lead yourself or anyone else into a sin against impurity. It means making sure others see you as God sees you—a precious and beautiful woman—not as an object to be used and abused for someone else's pleasure.

So how do you dress modestly?

1. Keep the "Bs" out of public view. The "Bs" are breasts, back, belly, and bottom.

2. Loosen up. Shirts so tight that buttons pop and bra lines show have got to go. So do pants and skirts that show the outline of your underwear, your bottom, and your hamstrings.

3. Don't keep it short. If when you bend over your skirt rides up so much that your rear end comes dangerously close to being in view, the skirt is too short.

4. Cover up. Shirts that look like lingerie should be used as lingerie. In other words, camisoles

are fine under sweaters, but not as stand-alone tops. Also, always keep your shoulders covered in church. You do not want your beauty to become a distraction from the beauty of Christ during the Mass.

"Sin does exactly the same thing to your spiritual vision that the wrong eyeglass prescription does to your physical vision. It corrupts how you understand truth. It blurs your vision of God, yourself, and others. It distorts your whole view of reality."

Discipline: The Practice of the Christian Life

If you want to get an A on a test, what do you do? You study. And if you want to be the star of the school play? You rehearse. How about the leading scorer on your basketball team? You practice.

Studying, rehearsing, practicing—you do all those things because success never comes without hard work. Whatever your goals are, they demand effort. They demand the concentrated application of your will. They demand discipline.

When you spend time every night doing your homework, reviewing your lines for the play, or practicing your free throws, you are being disciplined. You are training yourself to reach your goal. You're practicing self-control, denying yourself the opportunity to do things that might at the time seem more fun or interesting, but won't help you accomplish your ultimate goal.

Just like being valedictorian, nobody gets to become a saint without discipline. Holiness requires self-control. It requires that you do what you ought to do, even when you don't want to do it. This is one of the reasons Saint Paul compared sainthood to running a race. You have to practice, train hard, and push yourself all the way to the finish line. The only difference is that in the race to sainthood, the finish line isn't a blue ribbon. It's heaven.

Read

1. According to Romans 7:19–25, in our quest for holiness, what are we struggling against?

_____

_____

2. What does 1 Peter 1:13–16 say that we should set our sights on?

_____

_____

3. According to Proverbs 6:23, what way will discipline lead you along?

_____

_____

4. In Romans 8:12–18, what does Saint Paul say that it means to "live according to the flesh"? What happens to us if we live according to the flesh?

_____

_____

5. In that same passage, how does Saint Paul say those who live "according to the Spirit" should live? What must we do to be fellow "heirs" with Christ? What does that have to do with discipline?

_____

_____

6. Read the following passages. How does each describe the undisciplined life?

Proverbs 5:21–23 _____

Proverbs 25:28 _____

Psalm 50:16–23 _____

7. When you learn discipline, you learn self-control. That means you're better able to resist the temptations that can prevent you from reaching your goal. Jesus Himself modeled the importance of discipline in avoiding temptations.

_____

_____

Read the story of His temptation in the desert in Matthew 4:1–11. How did He prepare Himself to face that temptation?

_____

_____

8. Discipline can mean self-control. It also can mean doing certain actions that help you reach your goal. When it comes to getting to heaven, there are three essential actions or disciplines required of Christians: almsgiving, prayer, and fasting. During His life on earth, Jesus told us how to practice all three disciplines and what the benefit of doing so would be.

Read Matthew 6:1–20 and complete the chart below.

	How	Benefit
Almsgiving		
Prayer		
Fasting		

Reflect

1. Describe a goal you have accomplished in your lifetime. What did you do to reach that goal? Was reaching it hard or easy? Was the effort worth it?

_____

_____

2. How can you apply what you did to accomplish the goal you just described to your goal of becoming a saint?

_____

_____

3. Think back to how Scripture described the undisciplined life. Do any of those characteristics describe your own life? What things are you good at being disciplined about? In what areas do you still struggle?

_____

_____

_____

4. How do you think almsgiving, prayer, and fasting help us become saints? What lessons do they teach us?

_____

_____

5. On a scale of one to ten (ten being the best) evaluate how well you practice those three essential disciplines of the Christian life? Do you practice them often or rarely? What is your attitude while you practice them? How do you think practicing them more frequently or with a different attitude would help bring you closer to God?

_____

_____

_____

6. The way we spend and prioritize our time during the day has an important impact on our quest for holiness. Think about your day and how you spend your time. Do your days reflect your desire to get to heaven? If not, how can you spend your time differently? Are there some things you need to eliminate

from your schedule? Are there some things you need to add to your schedule? List both what can be added and what can be eliminated.

_____

_____

_____

Resolve

1. Practice a small act of self-renunciation each day by not hitting the snooze button on your alarm clock or by getting out of bed the first time your parents call you.

2. Set aside fifteen minutes at the same time each day for prayer. Block that time out in your schedule and plan other activities around it.

3. Every month, give away a portion of your allowance or paycheck to your parish or to a worthy charity.

MEMORY VERSE

"Therefore gird up your minds, be sober,
set your hope fully upon the grace that is coming to you
at the revelation of Jesus Christ."
1 Peter 1:13

"The way of perfection passes by way of the Cross. There is no holiness without renunciation and spiritual battle."

Catechism of the Catholic Church, 2015

MACKEREL SNAPPERS

Back when your grandparents were teenagers, Protestants (and some Catholics) referred to Catholics as "mackerel snappers." Why? Because at the time, all Catholics were obligated to give up meat every Friday, not just Fridays during Lent. By making that sacrifice, they were participating in some small way with the sacrifice Christ made on a Friday afternoon at Calvary.

Today, although giving up meat on Fridays is no longer mandatory, the Church still requires Catholics to offer up some small sacrifice in remembrance of Jesus suffering on Good Friday. If giving up meat on Fridays isn't in your family's meal plan, then try making some other small sacrifice every Friday—don't eat sweets, say an extra Rosary, or don't put salt on your food. Just make sure that whatever you do, you do it with a cheerful and willing spirit.

Grace Builds on Nature

What does making your bed every morning have to do with being a saint?

More than you think.

There's an old Catholic saying that "grace builds on nature." What that means is that the natural is the foundation for the supernatural. Or, in other words, it's your job to give God something to work with. You can choose to give Him a lazy, undisciplined, selfish heart or you can choose to give Him a hard-working, disciplined, selfless heart. He can do something with the former, but He will do a whole lot more with the latter.

So, what are some things you can do to learn discipline on the natural level that will make it easier for you to practice discipline on the supernatural level?

- Do your homework as soon as you get home from school and before you watch any TV or get on the computer. Don't put it off until bedtime or Sunday night.

- Start exercising. There was a reason Saint Paul always compared saints to athletes. The discipline you acquire from running, walking, swimming, or biking every day can help you do the hard things necessary for holiness.

- Get your body on a schedule. Go to bed at the same time and get up at the same time every day.

- And, of course, make your bed every morning (and keep the rest of your room clean as well).

Lesson 1: *Holiness 101*

READ

1. **A:** Keep the commandments.
2. **A:** Do not kill, do not commit adultery, do not steal, do not bear false witness, honor your father and mother, love your neighbor as yourself.
3. **A:** Sell his possessions and give to the poor.
4. **A:** Jesus was asking the young man to love God more than himself—to show God that He was more important than the riches and things of this life. This was difficult because the young man lacked the kind of love required to do what Jesus asked. He loved the things of this earth more than God.
5. **A:** The Pharisees were so concerned about following the letter of the Law and exterior faithfulness that they neglected the interior life and the more important matters: justice, mercy, and faith (Mt. 23:23).
6. **A:** Putting riches and things of this world before God; The devil; Love of the world.
7. **A:** Set our hearts right, be steadfast, make wise, careful decisions, and accept hardships; Be detached from the world; Work on developing the virtues of humility, prayer, and repentance; Hunger and thirst for righteousness; Keep alert for temptations to wrong and be sober, apply the truths of the faith to our lives, live simply, and ask someone to keep us accountable on our resolutions.
8. **A:** God is merciful and loves us unconditionally, which is why He saved us when we were still sinners and gave us the honor of sitting with His Son in heaven.

REFLECT

1–5. A: Answers will differ as they reflect your own personal situation.

Lesson 2: *The Dignity of Womanhood*

READ

1. **A:** Men and women are both made in the image and likeness of God. Together we share the responsibility of taking care of creation.

2. **A:** Before woman was created, there was no helper fit for man. She was created to be man's helper.

3. **A:** God took a bone out of Adam's side and from it created Eve. When Adam first saw her he was ecstatic, struck with awe at how perfectly suited to him she was, alike but different. Eve is called "woman" because she was taken out of man.

4. **A:** Woman is the "crown of Creation." The world was not complete without her. As man's helpmate, she is to be his partner, working with him in the tasks entrusted to them by God and making his efforts more fruitful than they would be if he were alone.

5. **A:** The beauty that these advertisements try to sell is only skin deep. It's fleeting, fading with time and age. The more we focus on that kind of beauty, the less we focus on real beauty that doesn't fade, the beauty of the spirit that comes through faith in God.

6. **A:** In the midst of a large crowd, Jesus told this woman that her faith had healed her and then held her faith up as an example to others; He pointed to this poor widow as the model of good behavior; Jesus spoke with the adulterous Samaritan woman, revealed to her the truths of His kingdom, and told her about the Messiah—in doing this, Jesus taught His apostles that He came to save everyone, even those who were sinners and who weren't Jewish, and that a woman could be entrusted with the important truths of God; He forgave the woman caught in adultery and showed her mercy when others weren't willing to do so.

7. **A:** Many women—Mary Magdalene, Mary the mother of James and Joseph, Salome; Mary Magdalene, Mary the mother of James and Joses, and many other women; Women

followers from Galilee; Mary, Jesus' mother, Mary's sister, wife of Clopas, Mary Magdalene, and the Apostle John.

8. **A:** John was the only apostle present at the Crucifixion. Women have a God–given gift for loving courageously, for loving even when it puts them in danger or when all the odds are against them.

9. Mary Magdalene. By making Mary Magdalene the "apostle of the apostles" (as John Paul II called her in his apostolic letter, *On the Dignity and Vocation of Women*), Jesus made it clear to the apostles that in His kingdom women were equal in dignity to men.

REFLECT

1–6. A: Answers will differ as they reflect your own personal situation.

Lesson 3: *Faith and the Life of Grace*

READ

1. **A:** Faith is the "assurance of things hoped for" and "conviction of things not seen."

2. **A:** It is granted to us. Only through the grace of God can we believe. Faith is a gift.

3. **A:** Without faith, it is "impossible to please" God.

4. **A:** No. We must both have faith and do God's will.

5. **A:** We must "eat His flesh and drink His blood." We do this every time we receive the Eucharist at Mass.

6. **A:**

Person(s)	Deed(s)
Abel	He offered an acceptable sacrifice; approved as righteous by God
Enoch	His faith pleased God and he was rewarded by being spared from death
Noah	He built an ark even though he had never seen rain
Abraham	He was called by God, went forth into the Land of Promise, not knowing where he was going; offered up his son Isaac, believing God could raise him from the dead
Sarah	She conceived a child in old age because she believed God would accomplish what He had promised
Isaac	He blessed Jacob and Esau
Jacob	He blessed the sons of Joseph
Joseph	Spoke of the Exodus and gave directions for his burial
Moses	He accepted abuse rather than be associated with sin, left Egypt, kept the Passover
The People of Israel	They crossed the Red Sea and did what God said to do in order to make the walls of Jericho fall.

Rahab	She welcomed spies and did not die
Gideon, Barak, Samson, Jephthah, David, Samuel, and the prophets	They conquered all kinds of evils.
Women and others	The dead were raised and others martyred

7. A:

	Mt. 15:21–28	Mk. 5:24–34	Lk. 1:26–38
What was the woman's faith in?	the power of Jesus to heal	the power of Jesus to heal	the power of God to accomplish the impossible
How did she show her faith?	she persistently called after Jesus and called Him "Lord"	she touched His robe believing that this would heal her	she believed the words of the angel and accepted the miracle to be done to her by God
What was God's response to her faith?	He proclaimed that she had faith and answered her request	He told her that her faith had healed her	He made her the Mother of God and the most blessed among creatures
How was her life different because of her faith?	her daughter was healed of the demonic possession	she was healed of her illness	she was the Mother of God and became the "Queen of Heaven"

REFLECT

1–6. A: Answers will differ as they reflect your own personal situation.

Lesson 4: *Love: To Serve Is to Reign*

READ

1. **A:** Everlasting love, continued faithfulness out of love; God loves us as He loves Jesus; While we were sinners, God loved us and died to save us; We are children of God and not slaves.

2. **A:** Tongues, prophecy, knowledge of mysteries, faith, almsgiving, and martyrdom.

3. **A:** Love is patient, kind, not jealous, not boastful, not arrogant or rude, does not act shamefully or seek its own interests, is not easily angered, does not think about wrongs done against them, is not happy with sin but rather with truth, love suffers, believes, hopes, endures all things, and never fails.

4. **A:** Fear, love, serve, and obey God; Love is the fulfillment of the Law so we are to love our neighbors as ourselves; Lay down our lives for our neighbors.

5. **A:** Faith showing itself through good works done out of love is the heart of the Christian faith.

6. **A:** Love one another as I have loved you.

7. **A:** Answers will vary but may include: Healing them, feeding them, correcting them, forgiving them, spending time with them, eating with them, teaching them, and suffering and dying for them.

8. **A:** She says yes to God, agreeing to do His will, not her own.

Reflect

1–6. **A:** Answers will differ as they reflect your own personal situation.

Lesson 5: *Prayer: The Way to a New Heart*
READ

1. **A:** At all times.

2. **A:** Ask, seek, and knock. We will receive what we ask for, find what we seek, and be answered when we knock.

3. **A:** We must search for Him with all our heart and all our soul.

4. **A:** The Lord promises to be near to those who pray to Him and give those who fear Him what they desire.

5. **A:** We should pray for each other to be healed. Our righteousness makes those prayers effective.

6. **A:**

	Luke 11:5–13	Luke 18:1–8	Luke 18:9–14
How are we to pray?	Consistently and persistently	Consistently and persistently	Humbly
What is the result of prayer?	We will get our heart's desire	God will not delay in answering us; we will be vindicated	Justication

7. **A:** 1. Praise and worship of God; 2. A request for God's will to be done and His kingdom to reign on earth; 3. Requests for our physical and material needs; 4. Requests for forgiveness and our spiritual needs.

8. **A:**

	Jesus' Prayer Life
When did Jesus pray?	Morning: All night
How did Jesus pray?	Three times He made the same request; conversationally spoke to the God the Father
Where did Jesus pray?	In a lonely place; on a mountain; in the wilderness; in the hills, in the Garden of Gethsemane
For what did Jesus pray?	God's will to be done; for Christians; protection from all evil; unity; our santification and eternal salvation

REFLECT

1–6. A: Answers will differ as they reflect your own personal situation.

Lesson 6: Obedience: The Proof of Our Love

READ

1. A: We will be saved and live with God in heaven.

2. A: We will not be rewarded with eternal life.

3. A: Keep His commandments.

4. A: They are not burdensome.

5. A: Obey God.

6. A:

	Blessings of Obedience
Isaiah 3:10	The fruit of our deeds on earth will be good.
John 15:10–11	In this world we will live in God's love and have joy.
James 1:25	Our actions in this life will be blessed.
2 Corinthians 5:10	We will receive rewards in heaven for the good we have done.
1 Peter 5:4	We will receive a crown of glory.
Revelation 22:12	God will repay us in heaven according to what we have done.
Revelation 22:14	We will again have the right to the tree of life (see Gen. 3).

7. A: Not God, but our own desires.

8. A: This temptation is not unique. Others have faced the same temptation before. God won't let us be tested by any temptation that is too strong for us to resist, and He will give us the grace we need to overcome the temptation if we ask for it and are willing to receive it.

9. A: a) The wife of Ananias; b) She did not honor a commitment she made to give the proceeds from a sale of her property to the Church; She lied about it and was struck dead; c) Peter told her that she and her husband tempted the Spirit and lied to God.

REFLECT

1–6. A: Answers will differ as they reflect your own personal situation.

Lesson 7: *Purity: The Way to See God*

READ

1. **A:** Someone who has clean hands, who does not lift their soul up (who does not give themselves) to something false, who does not swear deceitfully.

2. **A:** If we are pure, God will be able to use us for noble purposes.

3. **A:** We shall receive the gift of seeing God.

4. **A:** He is good to them.

5. **A:** He will rouse Himself for them and reward them.

6. **A:** Put to death what is earthly in us—immorality, impurity, passion, evil desires, covetousness, and idolatry.

7. **A:** Hope in God.

8. **A:** The Word of God.

9. **A:** Modestly, simply, sensibly, and with good deeds; Women should be submissive, reverent, and chaste, adorning ourselves with a gentle and quiet spirit; Women should be reverent, not slander others, not drink too much, be sensible, chaste, domestic, kind, and submissive.

REFLECT

1–6. **A:** Answers will differ as they reflect your own personal situation.

Lesson 8: *Discipline: The Practice of the Christian Life*
READ
1. **A:** Our own sinful nature.
2. **A:** The grace that is coming to us.
3. **A:** The way of life.
4. **A:** If a Christian lives according to the flesh, she lives according to her bodily passions and desires, she will die (not live in God's grace and not receive the gift of eternal life).
5. **A:** Those who live according to the Spirit are not slaves to sin. They put their sins to death. To be heirs with Christ we must suffer with Christ.
6. **A:** A sinful man will become a slave to his sin, and he will die; An undisciplined life is useless; God will disown the wicked and the undisciplined, while the disciplined will be saved.
7. **A:** Jesus fasted forty days and forty nights.
8. **A:**

	How	Benefit
Almsgiving	Give discreetly	God will reward you; teaches generosity, simplicity, sacrifice
Prayer	Pray discreetly, humbly	God will reward you; teaches humility, discipline, sacrifice
Fasting	Fast secretly; try to look your best so others will not know you're fasting.	God will reward you; teaches the body to submit to the will

REFLECT
1–6. A: Answers will differ as they reflect your own personal situation.